ABCDEFGHIJKLMNOPQRSTUVWXYZ

A
Family
Affair

ABCDEFGHIJKLM NOPQRSTUV WXYZ

A Family Affair

Pampoet

authorHOUSE®

AuthorHouse™
1663 Liberty Drive
Bloomington, IN 47403
www.authorhouse.com
Phone: 1-800-839-8640

Published by AuthorHouse   09/17/2012

ISBN: 978-1-4772-6495-9 (sc)

A Family Affair

I write because:

Habakkuk 2:2 And the Lord answered me and said, **"write"** . . .

I write because:

 Psalm 45:1 . . ."my tongue is the pen of a ready "**write**r."

I write because:

Ecclesiastes 3:1To everything there is a **season**, and a **time** to every purpose under the heaven: . . .

Born into poverty in Oakland, CA 1951; Pamela Ann Bowers the first girl of six boys. I acquired the love of the written word at the age of 12 when, for Christmas I was given a book of fables. Later in school I was introduced to poetry of which I acquired a keen liking. One of my favorite authors became Dr. Seuss.

I started writing poetry as something fun to do when giving gifts or for ones birthday. I went back and locate poems from the early 80's, some of which are within this first publication of some of my accumulative works. I have been writing poems off and on for over 30 years, never thinking one day I could or would become a published author.

I believe success comes from God and support from some earthly beings. I would like to acknowledge a few people who have encouraged and inspired me to write the book. After having been inspired from God to write over four years ago, I received a call from a dear Sister and friend Kimetta Coleman telling me," [I] had been disobedient to God as he had told [me] to write," I could do nothing but cry in agreement as I paid for the publication of this book over four years ago, but was never inspired to continue on with the publication of book. God told me to sell one of my copyrighted works, "Leaf of Thanksgiving Eve", for $20.00. (I have not done at this writing, but will.☺) as I said to myself," no one would pay $20.00 for a poem." I would like to give a shout-out to Mitzi as she is the one that gave me the needed $25.00 to get this poem copyrighted in 11/25/1997.

Another source of discouragement to me was when one of my children told me that I wrote like Dr. Seuss. I felt Dr. Seuss books were so elementary and child-like and received this statement in a negative light, until my dear Sister Kimetta ask me to listen to what I was saying, "**I wrote like Dr. Seuss**." We then laughed in agreement when she said, "could you use some Dr. Seuss money?" The greatest compliment and source of encouragement I could receive is when preparing poems for this book my youngest Granddaughter La'Trinity (aka Angel Baby) told me, after me having introduced to her to Dr. Seuss writings she said," Granny I like your poems better as I can understand them and they make more sense." These were the words of an eight year old! I have recently read the ears off my first Granddaughter Taylor (she has listened to all the poems as I edited them) and she, again, thinks Granny writes pretty well. My daughters Pam and Pat are ongoing sources of encouragement.

Other people who have always had my back along this journey are my best friend and Sister Rena (aka Corrine) who helped me with the editing and printing of many documents, her daughters Naomi, Deborah and Anna, Sister Amanda, Betty, Birdie, Monica, Octavia and Tonya, any names not mentioned charge to my head and not to my heart.

My husband and backbone, ***Bernard K. Botwe***: I love you!

Dedicated to

Esther Warner Franklin Bowers Morris

1926-2010

Acknowledgement

Willie, Cardella, Willie III (Destiny), Wayne, (Deaveon, Issac), Wesley, Edward, Melzena, Eddie, Antoine, Patrick, Pamela, Murphy, (Carl & Brian), C.J. (Trey), Malik, Taylor, Patricia, Jimmy, (Howard, Greg, Fred), Marquis, Hezekiah, La'Trinity, T.J. and Baby Q, Cassanda, Cayla, Curtis, Baby Curtis, Bernard Jr, Thelma, Roy, Greenfield, Athena,(Alvin, Alphonso), Micah, Kathy, Corrine, Ron,(Paul, Leon), Marcellis, Naomi, Angelo, Angelo Jr., Kaylani, Deborah, Paul, Kamari, Amanda, Greg, Kyle, Sister Bree, Pastor A. and L. Blackman. My Pastor and wife, Apostle Raymond & Pastor Octavia Dorrough, (Reule)of Love Christian Fellowship World Outreach Church: 409 East 10th Street, Pittsburg, CA 94565

CONTENTS

15 Days Before Christmas

T'was 15 days before Christmas I went to mail
The letter I received made me jump and yell

For a letter from Mom with money inside
I knew it was for me so I thought I would cry

When what to my wondering eyes should appear
But a itsy bitsy note that read Pamela dear

Give this money to each of the Great-Grandchildren real quick
So I got to the task lickety split

And I knew I could do this in spite of all else
I would send them a letter and clear up this mess

So on Willie III and Wayne and Wesley
On Edward Jr and Antoine and Patrick make three

On C.J. and Malik and Princess Taylor of course
And Marquis and Hezekiah all Grandsons of choice

And I heard your Great-Grand say "out of place but not sight"
A blessed Christmas to you all and to you all a blessed LIFE

Made especially for you 11 wonderful Grandchildren:
By Granny Pam aka pampoet
December 10, 2002
Made for **Great Grand-Ma Esther Franklin**

722

722 Is the number for US
This is a love that really is a must

722 you took my hand
Said, "that you would be my man"

722 What are you going to do?
Capture all my hopes, make my dreams come true

722 Took a good look at you
Now you know I am no fool

722 Has come and gone
You disappeared left me all alone

722 The day WE wed
God ordained it a Holy Bed

722 turned upside down
While you could have been happy, you left with a frown

722 Is drawing near
God has allowed me to call you dear

722 Will be TEN & TWENTY years
Since we said "I Do" no longer have we fears

722 I said "I Do"
Always promise to be faithful to you

722 Eddie and Melzena's 10th Anniversary
God has blessed them to make marital history

722 Pam & Q will be one
As Q has decided to be Christ Son

722 Will come and go
But love for each other will continue to grow

10/29

(2009)
It has now been some time
Since this dear man left me in a bind

As on this day God called him away
Leaving behind his Granddaughter Tay

He was loved until the end
My high-school sweetheart, lover husband and friend

09/10
Here we go again
But Eddie and Melzena are now just friends

As marriage they no longer have
Three beautiful grandsons that make me glad

They stayed married longer than most
Thank God for the Father, Son and Holy Ghost

A Daughter Named Athena

I have a daughter named Athena and she is a star
She did a lot of traveling without her own car

For she did not pass the test they say
She did not give up she just began to pray

She went here and she went there
She even managed to change her hair

She got married to a wonderful man
A man who Athena he did understand

For I have a daughter named Athena and she is a star
She did a lot of traveling without her own car

She went to visit her husband far away
Knowing one day at home with her he would stay

She got a promotion on her job
That is because she stayed close to her God

And then a new apartment she received
This girl is awesome can you believe

And then one day after she did pray
She passed that driving test any old way

Cause I have a daughter named Athena she is a star
And now she is driving her own new car

March 15, 2000
copyright@P.A.M./tm/Pamela Qualls
Made especially for Athena

A House Is Not A Home

A house is not a home
When there are people inside and still you are alone

There are 3 people in this house
So why is it as quiet as a mouse?

Because, a house is not a home
When there are people inside and still you are alone

You want to talk, communicate
But for you it is too late

As one of the people cannot hear
And the other always says, "get away from here."

A house is not a home
When there are people inside and still you are alone

You try to do everything that you can
To love the woman and stand by the man

But instead of getting love and respect
You get talked down to this I will bet

He says that he is perfect and close to the Lord
Can't prove it by me let that go on record

As a house is not a home
When there are people inside and still you are alone
Created 12-31-08
4:30a.m.

Many times in life we acquire all the many things in life that we strive so
hard for only to find out that the house that you have filled with stuff is
not a home. As a home is where peace and serenity should be. A home
should be your safe haven from the world. So do not allow your "home"
to be just a house. Make sure your house is a home, where the spirit of
the Lord loves to come and roam.

A Late Valentine

Dearest Son Alvin, I thought it was time
For me to sit down and send you this valentine

It has been a few years, trying to send this card
But with God on our side nothing is hard

So I tore it a part and that is a start
To getting it to you as you are dear to my heart

I am sending a little change inside
Twenty dollars is not much maybe next time I'll send twenty-five

My blessed Son your card I did receive
I intended to send you a response with speed

But you know that this Mom is always on the go
But I have to take time to let you know

Not a day goes by that I do not pray
Lord bring my son home, do it any kind of way

Prison doors (God) can open shut doors too
Just keep believing and he will rescue you

So all my love I send your way
Please be blessed on this Patrick's 7th Birthday

Made by Pamela Qualls especially
for my son: Alvin

March 9, 2004
March 30, 2004 was C.J.'s BD he is now 14 (Pam's son)
Bay Point, Ca 94565

I had sent my son (spiritual son) a huge valentine card for Valentine's
Day only for it to be returned to me as to large to be received at the
institution. So it took me almost a year to finally figure out how to send
the card to him, I had to cut it into forth's and that way I was able to
send him the Valentine Card.

A Mother's Day Tribute To Willie Jr.

Son it has taken you 30 years
For your family to call you dear

For you my son you are taking us back in time
To a place where life was happy and all was fine

For off to Clearlake all your family is going
We all will have fun this we all are knowing

For as Eddie and I were talking yesterday
This is a place in time he wished we could stay

Willie I thank God for you
A legacy for all is what this week-end will do

For your son Wayne's 9th Birthday is the cause
That this Mother on Mother's day can sit back and take pause

Thank you for Jr. remembering this place
And bringing a smile to your brother and sisters face

As this was a place of much fun and love
We can thank Grandpa Murphy(E.V.)and our Father above

So this Mothers Day it is all because of you.
That all my children will be with me and I won't be blue

Jr. we all love you this is true
It does not matter what you may do

You are the oldest brother of four
And we just want to love you and not keep score

TO MY OLDEST SON
WILLIE JR.
May 9, 1999
pampoet
When I was married to the children's father Willie his parents Ernest and
Gladys always took the grands to Clearlake for fishing. My son passed
this legacy on to his Sons.

A Sister Named Rachell

I have a sister named Rachelle
She works in an office and not in a cell

She quit her job and put in her all
In the purpose of her call

See God called her to a business of her own
I would not be easy long hours on the phone

She has a purpose and she has a plan
As long as she does not faint but continues to stand

She comes to work early and goes home late
But this dear Sister has an important date

Date to be successful in her endeavor
To sell her business real soon to whoever

So if you know someone out there who wants to buy?
Bring them to Rachell and she will tell them why!

Why she is focused and uses no dope
Why she is encouraged and filled with hope

Why she keeps her head to the grind
Why she works hard and that is no crime

So come on by and say, "hello"
She is located near the Marina on Railroad

I am an entrepreneurial and at one time in the later part of 199?
I had an office on 4th and Railroad in Pittsburg, CA
The office next door was a young women who was making software
For African American clip art, we lost contact? If you know her let her
know, I did not forget her!

ABC'S For Antoine's Birthday
Number "7" Seven

Antoine today is your special day
Birthday so you can come out and play
C.J. and all the kin will come
Dogs and chips it is sure to be fun
Eating up food with all your family
Feeding us all what a sight to see
Granny is coming on the scene
Harry(Granpa) is here, he is nice not mean
I am a poet and this is true
Just keep on reading and you'll know it too
Kids are coming from everywhere
Lajuan and Leonard are sure to be there
Maybe Alisha because they all care
Na"knee"nana is sure to come
Open your gifts I'm sure she brought you one
Pawpaw may happen on the scene
Quick as can be for your party he will sing
Rest assured there is money in this card
Saved my money and it was hard
Today I give you $5 x 7
Unless I counted wrong you are seven not eleven
Vision all the savings in the bank you will have
When Christmas comes around and you will be glad
X-tra things you can get
You are saving your money this I bet
Zero in on the savings plan
You my Grandson will have money in your hand

ABC'S OF C.J.'S 10TH Birthday

As always now is the time
To make a poem for you and it has to rhyme
Because today your are now 10
C.J. is Grannies special friend
Did not get to your party on time
Everyone knows I was kinda in a bind
First I had to go to the bank
Get fifty dollars $50.00 what do you thank
Harry (Granpa) was working on the car
I was trying to become a star
Just as time kept ticking on
Kids are everywhere having fun
Last but not least I'm on my way
Making a poem what can I say
Now your day should be almost over
Open your gifts not a four-leaf-clover
Pam-Pam your Mom worked real hard
Quickly setting up in the yard
Rushing to get there I'm on my way
Started off earlier on this day
Took off to pick up the van
Up on railroad by the stand
Van is spotless for your day
What my grandson have you to say
X-tra fun is what I want you to do
You are grandson number two "2"
Zero is the last letter of the alphabet
Your going to have a great party this I bet
Love always: Big Gran

ABC's For Wesley 8ᵗʰ. Birthday

As you can see I am a little bit late
Birthday for you was not at Clearlake
Cake and ice cream I did not have
Did not know it would make you sad
Each and every year you and I share this day
For you are my special birthday Boy! I say hooray!
Glad you were born just for me
Happy I am you are one of the W threes
I owe you some money and I am going to pay
Just as soon as I see another payday
Keep on growing and getting big and strong
Looking in the mirror you see you belong
Must be nice sharing a birthday with me
Now your are 8 no longer three
Open your envelope and you will see
Pretty five dollar bills 8 exactly
Quarters are good but dollars are better
Remember to save as you read this letter
Save a little her and a little bit there
Then in November you will know all is fair
U are suppose to send your money to the bank
Vault is safe and monies in a tank
Wesley is my number 5 grandson
X-tra special now I gotta run
You are the apple of my eye
Zero, Wesley as I say good-by

---

made especially for you, by your Big Gran: Pampoet on July 23, 2000

Adam And Eve

A woman lying with a woman, she should be dead
Man lying with a man, dead is what the Word said

This is a situation that should not be
Jesus said,"you must come to me"

God created man by a plan
Made a woman to help man stand

If it don't fit don't force it is a song
But consider what the song is as you journey along

God created Adam and said,"that he was good"
Needed him a woman so that he could do as he would

Then Adam needed companionship
God gave him Eve someone that wears a slip

The whole purpose of man was to pro-create
With a woman this was his perfect mate

What can a man and a man do
Not what God intended with a woman too!

Can a man lay on a man's soft and firm breast
Soothe his mind help him rest

Can a woman's embrace be strong
With a woman this is all wrong

Now if you do not understand what I am trying to say
Take heed to the words I've written this day

If you are a man and a little confused
Then what I'm about to tell you will be good news

God made a womb-man because she was a man with a womb
If you do not have a womb my brother then you can be in tuned

In-tuned with yourself and the man you are
Give it over to Jesus Sir, and you can still be a star

Afraid

Lean not to thine own understanding that's what the good Book SAID
For the things that you don't understand will have you always AFRAID

Afraid of where you're going to GO
Afraid of people you don't even KNOW

Afraid to be submissive to your MAN
Afraid to believe you're in God's HAND

Afraid to Kill old jealousy and STRIFE
Acting that way you'll never become a WIFE

Afraid that when you turn AWAY
Someone else will steal your PLAY

So don't be afraid don't try to UNDERSTAND
Just put your trust in the creator and in your MAN
12-02-84

Angel Baby

Our Angel Baby is built like a brick house
She is beautiful she's agile she is swift like a mouse!

She has a house that is beautiful and clean
Curves and body that would make anyone beam

Angel Baby is not 20 but three
Lord have mercy how can this be?

She is solid she is sturdy a block stopper guaranteed
What in the world does all of this mean?

She has a shape from her mother and brains from her Dad
This is the smartest little Angel a Granny ever had

So we will pray and keep the wolves away
As her house is sacred, all the fellows stay at bay

Angel Baby is my second granddaughter. My story is that God looked around heaven and sent us a Princess named Taylor, then when it was time for my second granddaughter to arrive all the Princess were gone so he grabbed me an Angel and sent her down with the name of La'Trinity. Granny dubbed her "Angel Baby". This poor little girl who is now 8 years old and looks every bit of 10 with the shape of a 20 year old. Lord have mercy.

Athena's Grandest Birthday

March 27th 1998

This is your special day
Look up and say," hooray"
For Satan tried to take your day
At your birth you were not O.K.

You were not breathing when you came out
Doctors said, "what is this all about?"
Cerebral Palsy is its name
Steal you oxygen, mess with your brain

Make your joints kind of stiff
Make it hard for you to lift
Lifted your head up to the sky
Thank God almighty his healing passed by

By his stripes you were healed
You have climbed many challenging hills
You could say life gave you a bitter pill
You could lay around and just be ill

But you choose to have a grand life
Married Alvin and now you are his wife
Got a promotion on your job
You deserved it you work real hard

You don't complain you keep on going
God is always good this you are knowing
27th year will never come again
Just enjoy this day smile and grin

God knew you formed in your mother's womb
Satan thought that would be your tomb
God made you special so you could say
God thank you for my life on this my Grandest Birthday

Athena is my spiritual daughter she is my oldest daughter's best friend, I
have know her since high school!

Be My Friend

Be my friend is what he said!
As I allowed this to sink into my head.

I cannot be true to my race
If I let this white man into the secret place

Place were hopes and dreams are made.
Made me understand why I was afraid

Afraid to face up to the truth
Truth that white grapes also make good juice

Juice that runs deep in our veins
Veins of life and hope and pain

Pain to know we all bleed blood
Blood was shed from him above

Above all colors and powers that be
God made Earl first and then he made me

Pamela Qualls

I met a most wonderful man named Earl after praying for God to send me a man to love me as I always love. Earl bowled into my life and we began a one year relationship. He was the most wonderful man to me and my children, the only problem was that he is white and I am black. I could not get over this fact. God had sent the best man for me, but I refused because it did not come in the package that I was looking for. My loss!

Beginning And End Of Yellow Cadillac

This is a true story of a guy a girl, and their car.

Yellow Cadillac so bright
Shimmering, glistening in the light

Brand new rolling off the lot
You my dear were hot, hot, hot

Then the cares of life beat you down
Down to wobbling all over town

Then the hubcaps you used on your shoes
Were stolen one night, gave you the blues

But still to your lady's house you go
Rickety, sickity up Leland Road

Rollin, profilin, leaning and all
Yellow Cadillac you knew you were tall

Tall as a soldier in a war
Driving your lady to the grocery store

Store all these memories in your heart
Yellow Cadillac we had to part

This is a true story of a young man that was courting his girl. He knew
he was cool as he had this little raggedy Cadillac that appeared to be
dying in front of his eyes. He was still very proud of this car and drove his
girl all over town with only one door that opened.

Belated 13th. Birthday Willie III

Willie your birthday has come and gone
But thoughts of you still linger on

As on your birthday Gran was broke
But that's all right God loves broke folk

For July 17th owed you some green
You are 13 years old, know what I mean

Five dollars times thirteen equals 65
It took a little time to pull it together and Grandson that is no jive

But the time has finally come
So now I can pay up, Grandson have fun

Save your money is the test
You can win at this game I'd truly bet

Save a little here, and a little there
This time next year you will be rich I do declare

So Gran enjoyed going to your class
Saying Happy Birthday it was a blast

Grandson in college at the age of thirteen
He is a scholar, his sharp and clean

I love you now and I love you then
Always think of Granny as you best friend

Made especially for you by your Gran
Pamela Qualls
August 20, 2000

You spent the night at her house and went to a picnic
Willie III is my first grandson of 12, he was the apple of every ones
eyes for the first three to five years of his life, then
the other grandsons came like rabbits, by his 10th
Birthday there were 10 grandsons. So this my first has had
some challenges, though quite intelligent as
he was in an advanced math class at L.M.C. when he was 13.
When all the family kicked him to the curb, his granny was there for him
again, and again.
I am happy to say at this writing he is doing quite well
Love you: Poopy☺

Birth Of Baby Eddie

There once was boy named Eddie
Who was born in a far away city

He was born during a storm
The weather was not warm

In fact he was born during a blizzard;
We didn't know how he would be delivered

See it was during time of war,
In 1991 and not 1994

The war was called Desert Storm
Granny was gonna stay at home

But Melz said," Mom please come
Without you here it will not be fun

So Granny prayed and took a jet,
The Lord has never failed her yet

And when I got there the babe was not born,
We did go bowling in the midst of a storm

Then over in the night
Melzena awoke with a fright

She said, Mom it is time
For the birth of this baby of mine

Off to the hospital we ran,
Eddie was stationed in Germany land

The labor was hard,
We kept God on his guard

And finally on Feb. 13th
Eddie was born with scream

See he was in the oven to long,
This didn't make us sing a happy song

So he was air lifted to Trier
There were baby specialists there

He was in the hospital for a week
See he was sick and very weak

He swallowed his insides
Called meconium, and this no lie

Then Baby Eddie came home,
Granny again was airborne

Today Eddie is seven "7",
a blessing from heaven

He is grandson number four,
Thank God his life Melz did bore

His name is steady Eddie to me
Now that is the story of Baby Eddie

Baby Eddies is my forth grandson, he was born during a snow storm
Most all the medical staff was away at war, so his mother was in labor for
Almost a full day with continuous pushing, so when the baby was born after
Such a long time of trying to come into the world,
he swallowed the meconium
Was deathly ill and was airborne to children's hospital in Germany. It was
really funny as when we went to visit him, the nurses and doctors knew who
we were coming to visit, as we were the only Black people in the hospital.

Bodies Laying Everywhere

Bodies laying everywhere
All they do is lay and stare

She has a man who really loves the Lord
All they need is to get on one accord

A body here, a body there
There seems to be bodies everywhere

Her man gives her a REASON to smile
Although she has not seen him for a while
As he has to pick up another body now

Bodies laying everywhere
All they do is lay and stare

He runs here he runs there
Gotta pick up a body, there everywhere

Her man has a REASON to complain
He has to pick up bodies in the rain

There is never a time or a place
That her man is not looking at another dead face

So while her REASON has health and life
Her prayer is to someday be his wife

Bodies laying everywhere
All they do is look and stare

04/99
COPYRIGHT@Pamela Adkins-Murphy
This poem was inspired by a lady that was dating a mortician.

Born Again

So you ask me if I am Born Again
This is my answer to you my friend
Living for Jesus is nothing but a win
No more enjoying the pleasures of sin

Born Again is a way of Love
Shown to us from our Father above
He sent his son who gave his life
No more anger, suffering or strife

Born Again "oh yes" I am
God gave me a name and that is Pam I Am
P.owerful A.nd Mighty nChrist is what I do
Cause I know Jesus loves me and he loves you too

So if you want to be a part of the Born Again crew
Read real closely I will tell you what to do
Ask him to come into your life
Confess with your mouth do away with strife
Believe in your heart Christ was raised from the dead
The same shall be saved is what the word said

So now that you are Born Again
You are my Sister, my brother my friend
www.allpoetry.com

If you would like to be born again this poem is a beginning.
Written January 21st, 2006

Bring Back The "Golden Rules"

Have you been looking at the news?
No one seems to know the "Golden Rules"

He said it plainly in his Word
You should not even hurt a bird

But I read where child shots child with a gun
How did all of this begun

It began when prayer was removed from school
Said, the Ten Commandments were all to cruel

Did not want the children to write "Thou Shalt Not Kill"
Did want them to take a birth control pill

Did not want them to quote "Thou shalt not steal"
Did want them to think having their own mind a good deal

Did not want them to know to obey their parents, their days
would be long
Did want them to know in prison they would belong

Did not want them to know the one and true God
Did want them to join gangs and when older a mob

Did not want them to know not to worship graven image
Now they get tattoos, piercing and all for new image

Did not want them to tell the truth
Don't bear false witness another of the rules

Said all of this infringed upon their rights
Now the violence from children is out of sight

Child abuse is out of hand
Society needs to take a stand

Put prayer and bibles back in school
Begin to teach them the "Golden Rules"

Then they will learn love and respect
God will forgive he's never failed America yet

Busy Day

You got out of bed this morning
And kneeled down quickly to pray
You were in a hurry
Even though Christ had some things to say

Then you got real busy
As you ran by him and her
Will they even remember you
Or were you just a blur?

The day is almost over
And your labor for this day is through
Is there anyone that can utter
A kind word for you

Can you say at night
As you arrive at home
Lord I gave someone a smile
So they did not feel alone

Did you take time and give
Someone a reason to live?
Or did you just run through your day
Not taking out time to pray

Possibly someone hopes were fading
Did you encourage them to look a head?
Or did you rush right by them
In a hurry to get home and to your bed

Is anyone rejoicing by what you did or said
Or do they feel the world would be a better place
If people like you were dead?

Whatever seeds you sowed today will bring you joy or sorrow
So as the day comes to an end, don't worry about tomorrow

COPYRIGHT@P.A.M.
03-24-98
Pamela Adkins-Murphy

Car Gone

I went to get into my car today

It was not there someone had taken it **away**

Away to where I do not know

But God knows all and in this he will **show**

Show how all my needs he will provide

For now I must walk and later I can **ride**

Ride to tell what God has **done**

Done blessed my life with another one

Cars may come and cars may go

Remember God is good I told you so

This Sunday morning in 2000, I had cooked dinner for our church and also had clothing that I was going to give to the ministry for our clothing give away, however; thinking my car was stolen only to discover, it was repossessed. I would like to say that since that time God has blessed me with many, and various forms of transportation from a 15 passenger van (for the grandchildren) to a brand new 2008 Chevrolet, Impala.

Published in: Falling Rain
VIP P2207153-999
Pamela Qualls
www.poetry.com

Cinnamon Roll

Why does Jesus love me so?
He loves me down to the **_cinnamon roll_**

Neighbor just called me on the phone
Wanting to know if I was home

Had something for me that was oh so sweet
When I got it made my knees go weak

As I had just said to the "Lord"
I need cinnamon rolls that right now I cannot afford

Donna had a pack of cinnamon rolls handed to me
Can you see how God will take care of thee

So Jesus loves me this I know
Cause he loves me down to the **_Cinnamon roll_**

Inspired by next door neighbor: Donna who has been an Angel in disguise to me. I had no one to help me move and she stepped in and did most of it with me and for me. May God forever bless her as she has so generously blessed this child of God! The morning of this poem I had wanted to invite Donna over for coffee and cinnamon roll as this is something I had started doing, but when I looked I only one cinnamon roll left in the pack, and after making coffee anyway, Donna called and brought me a pack of rolls the exact same brand and kind that I had been sharing with her.

Pampoet aka Pamela Botwe
February 3, 2011

Contest: Why I Need A Laptop?

As 18th of Dec. I lost my Mom a part of Gods plan
But now it is hard for me to stand

I am home-bound and need a way out
With a laptop I can go out and about

Out on the inter-net about to be discovered
I am an entrepreneurial poet and like me there is no other

I would be able to produce my poetry book
Others can interface with me and take a look

A new laptop would make me oh-so-glad
As the old one was Dell and it is sad

So help this senior get into the swing
By winning a Mac or HP you know what I mean

Jan 2010 by pampoet aka Pamela Qualls Botwe

Cost Of Love!

What is the COST OF LOVE you say?
Come along I will explain it today

Love is patient and always kind
This kind of love is hard to find

More than silver, more precious than gold
When you pay the COST OF LOVE, you'll have and hold

Hold onto love no matter what the cost
For if you turn love away you will be lost

Love does not care who is the boss
For in perfected love there is no loss

So when you pay the COST OF LOVE
Make sure the cost is from above

You will never experience pain
When you are willing to start over again

When the COST OF LOVE is pure,
COST OF LOVE will be your cure

COST OF LOVE

pampoet©July 30, 2009
Accra, Ghana/West Africa
In the home of the my fiancé Bernard K. Botwe

Daeveon

07-26-11

Daeveon, Daeveon how could this be?

You are no longer 2 as today you are 3

Great Granny Pam came to share your day

Cause she loves you would not have it any other way

You and Destiny are the best of friends

And with that said, this poem will end!

Made especially for you by Granny

pampoet 07-30-11

Dating On Line

On the Internet I requested a brother
Only because I think they are better than the other

And then one day to my surprise
On the Internet I got my reply

His lines were sweet, his diction real fine
Would this be the man, I would make mine?

For the Word does say that a man that finds
Will end up with a pure gold mine

For a Lady is in a class of her own
This man did call me on the phone

With fear and apprehension we did talk
My situation in life he did not balk

He's kind, He's' warm, He's loving He's true
And then he said, "his eyes were **BLUE**

To my shock and my surprise
This for me I had to apprise

And after trying to deny this man
He reached through the screen and took my hand

Color should not be an issue here
He wants a Lady who will not fear

Fear to allow God to change her life
And possibly become this WHITE mans wife

For his name may be Earl
And there is much value in a
White Pearl

copyright@Pamela Adkins-Murphy
April 18, 1999

Easter Morn

I was awaken this Easter morn
By Antoine's sweet little voice on the telephone

Happy Easter is what he said
As I rejoiced laying on my bed

Then my son Eddie came on the phone
Said, Mom I'll be over if you're gonna be home

Look at some movies is what we can do
Didn't want his Mom feeling lonely and blue

So this Easter already I am blessed
As I must stay home off my feet and rest

So Eddie did come knocked at my door
Had a pink rose and strawberries from the store

A breakfast for him I did not fix
He came to my house at noon not six

So off to Denny's we did go to eat
So I didn't have to cook and be on my feet

After having a lot of fun
Home he went as he had to run

So I thank God for my baby Boy
He is such a wonderful Son and my great joy

Easter Sunday April 4, 1999
I had just had two major surgeries the end of 1998
and the first part of 1999
So I was still in the recovery stages.

Evening Walk

This evening I went a walking
Keys in hand was not talking

As I began to go home, the dark did befall me
As I looked before me a hooded guy I did see

Do not get it wrong as this Granny knows how to brawl
So as I was at the ready approaching him I saw

My baby Patrick walking all handsome, smiling and tall
This was my younger grandson I knew, he would not let me fall

Said,"Dad said I should come, and get you out here walking all
alone".
Told,"him no need to worry I had my cell phone"

So Love is more than words, it is action I did see
That my son Eddie loves his Mom, and this Mom loves her son
Eddie.

While I was staying at my son Eddies home, I decided to go for a walk
late in the evening, as I began to walk back home it began to get dark.
My wonderful son sent one of my younger Grandsons Patrick to come
and check on me. I do love me some Patty Wat☺

Fa-la-la-la-la-la-la-la-la

Now that the Christmas season is here
I have a few questions-Please don't fear

For the stores are crowded from door to door
With busy shoppers running across the floor

The children are screaming everywhere I go
Why do prices go up ?Why is this line so slow

Where's Saint Nick-?-Who use to hang around
All we have on the corners are-kids" breakin down"

What happened to the Christmas trees with all the gold & glitter
It really doesn't matter because after the 1st, it's all pine litter

Do you her Christmas Carols singing through the air
No I hear "Soul Music", doesn't anyone care?

What happened to baby Jesus lying in a manger?
To those who forgot-He's just another stranger

We've lost respect for the old times
Advancements & Movements have numbed our little minds

Let's all stop & think from this refrain
Now facing reality not to complain

So think about the pass of how Christmas became
Not the lies of Santa the reindeers so tame

But the birth of Jesus Christ-In a stable far away
To later die for the sins of the world on another "Holiday"

---

copyright@Pamela Adkins-Murphy/tm/P.A.M
This poem was ***written by my adopted-spiritual son***
(Pepe) during the Christmas season of 1984.

Fathers Its Time To Come Out Of Your Comatose State

Stop blaming your Mother or Father for your mistakes
Hurry and come out of that comatose state

You wonder why your kids head is so hard
Possibly because of you they are always on their guard

They want discipline, love and respect
They are waiting on your fathers, you haven't come through yet

Men come out of your comatose state, take a spiritual pill
It's time for you to get busy on a house for God to build

Our heavenly Father all he did was give
Gave his precious Son Jesus so that we could now live

Any man can make a child
Father is one who sticks around for a while

There are so many angry children in the land
Because Fathers are not there leading them by their hand

Fathers today want to be cool
They should be living by the golden rule

By precept and example is the way you should live
Time and attention to your child you should give

Fathers come out of your comatose state
For what you do now will seal your children's fate

Children are hurting because fathers are not there
They need to know that their fathers really care

Children need to know they can count on you
So they won't have to always be nervous, disturbed and feeling blue

Study your children and then you will know
What's inside of them as you watch them grow?
Father's Day Message: June 21, 1998

First Born

You were born the first born son
Had five brothers I was the only one

Only girl standing all alone
Being the older brother I know was not much fun

Misunderstood most all of the time
That was a shame a sin and a crime

But we won't let Satan; in and win this time
We are entering our golden years and doing just fine

For it has taken us 50 years to get to this date
Where we can come together and celebrate

Celebrate your life that was given
Celebrate the fact that your still "livin"

So let us not fuss and let us not fight
Trust in God we will do alright

We are going to keep Love in our hearts
As you will always be my brother and so we start

Start to mend the hurts of the past
Forever looking forward
Loving Brother and sister at last

copyright@Pamela A. Qualls aka pampoet
Made especially for my Oldest Brother:
Warner
May 5, 2002

He is 52 Years and 10 months old today (July 5th).
I love you brother and may God bless you to see 50 + more.

First Year Anniversary

August 14, 1999-2000

Our first year anniversary is drawing near
I love it when you answer me"yes dear"

I do not know what plans you may have
But I'm sure whatever will make me glad

Glad you came back into my life
Said "God sent you back to reclaim your wife"

Open your spiritual eyes and you will see
All the blessing God has just waiting for thee

If you will listen to me, we will grow
Just remember I tried to tell you so

So a wife God gave you; you now have
What are you going to do to make her glad?

I need a man to rub my neck
Take time to love me and give me respect

I want you to caress my breast
Hold me in your arms at night and let me rest

Open up your Bible and talk about the Lord
You must walk with God let this be put on record

Marriages are not made stable because you said so
They are build upon with lots of love just like a flower grows

You tend to it you nurture it and then you get a bloom
It's kinda what I'm looking for when you came to be my groom

I want to blossom and to bloom
I love having you in my room

Turn off the TV and spend some time
Then you can say I will always be a wife of thine

made especially for you Q
Pamela Qualls aka pampoet

Gemini

Gemini deals with ideas, principles and ABSTRACTIONS
Whenever a twin is around it's quite an ATTRACTION

Gemini is a restless SIGN
He forever has many things on his MIND

It is difficult for him to be STILL
He must be moving or he might miss that DEAL

Gemini always wants to know WHY?
He'll keep at it till he figures it out by and BY

Gemini usually understands most THINGS
Like how things operate and what makes birds SING

They have a problem making up their MINDS
They'll say one thing now and change it next TIME

Don't forget this is the sign of the TWIN
Two against one you'll never WIN

A Gemini's mind thinks real FAST
For Mr. Gemini this is an Easy TASK

Gemini must be allowed to be FREE
He must be on the move possibly to the SEA

Gemini is loyal to principle and DESIGN
He doesn't consider people unless there in a BIND

They are a lot of fun don't get me WRONG
They'll have you laughing all day LONG

So in conclusion what I SAY
Two are better than one ANYWAY

Pampoet

Gift From God

You bring them into the world
Sometimes it's a boy sometime it's a girl

You have a lot of hopes and dreams
You pray they will be kind to you and never mean

Your there when they coo, your there when they cry
Your always there beside them to wipe their little eye

You watch them take their very first step
As you are their safety net

You don't let them fall
Now they walk real tall

You see them hit their first ball
You watch them hold their first doll

You watch them as they become of age
You see them as they graduate

Oh! You are so proud
Then they say, you are to loud

You speak of them from state to state
They continue to tell you all about your mistakes

You try to get them to understand
They shove you away; they don't want to hold your hand

You want to hold them, wipe their tears
They won't let you touch them it goes on through the years

You love them unconditionally
Whether it's a she or a he
Children are a gift from God
Sometime you have to just let them be

Girls We Are Loved

When I was just a little girl
Hair combed neatly sometimes a braid sometimes a curl

I did not have a father to love☹
Then I got in touch with the father above☺

Did not have a father to hold my hand
Did not have a father to help me understand
Did not have a father to show me a real man

And then the father up above came and gave us perfected love

Jesus gave his life for me
Save my soul and set me free
Free to know who really loved me
Our heavenly father the creature of WE

Glaucoma

The doctor told me I'm going blind

Said," high pressure in my eye not one of a kind"

Glaucoma is the name of this terrible disease

What it does for me is take me to my knees

As God is a healer this I know

Gonna heal my eyes then I will show

Show how he healed my eyes and then

I can keep on playing games with my friends

I cherish my eyes just like my song

Satan trying to take them, better go where he belong

Cause I use my eyes each and every day

I love to read, but don't need them to pray

So come on Glaucoma get thee away

I need my eyes each and every day

Written 04/12/03 I sit here today July 31, 2012
Free from glaucoma and diabetes as God is a healer.

Godfather C. Henderson 85th Birthday

What you are looking at is a picture of all the clan
You do not see me on there as I am Pam I am

I live behind the camera and so I can't be seen
But visualize me on that picture, see me, I am clean

But I wanted your day to be special, as you are dear to me
We all got together; everyone on the pictures is almost here with
thee

Sandra is way in Texas and I don't know if Charles can come
John John may be here late but, you know he will be here on
the run

Then there is Paul and Rena and of course all of the girls
These Granddaughters are most beautiful as pretty as priceless
pearls

And Nancy J. is on her way you know you can depend
She is just as close to us as any family kin

So Papa know that I love you and all of my crew do to
Harry is your newest son and he help cut chicken too

Kick back eat, relax and enjoy the cake your Sister made
You know Aunt Carrie is the one that compliments are paid

Your greens were cooked by Auntie Mable
And your niece Tommie decorated your table

So stay around for 10 more years
We will do this again just have no fear

Pamela Qualls
June 16, 2000
My Godfather has gone on to be with the Lord☹

Going Blind

Today the doctor told me your going blind
Said," pressure in your eyes not in your mind"

Whose report am I going to believe?
Gonna believe the Lord stay on my knees

Gonna use these eyes just as sure as can be
Gonna play my games cause I can see

What would it be like without my sight?
Don't even want to know gives me a fright

He said in his Word, "blinded eyes they would see"
That right there is enough faith for me

For without faith it is impossible to please
I have the faith so I know I will see

There's a great big world for me to see
So keeping the faith, I'll just let it be

This poem was written over 12 years ago (04/12/2003), and since that time God totally healed me from glaucoma and diabetes. And there is a big world for me to see as he sent me to Africa where I married the love of my life: Bernard☺

G. Household

1998

There once was a guy named Brian
Brian was always found tryin

Tryin to please his wife named Pam
Not taking green eggs and ham

Now that is a guy name Brian

One day they had a son named Malik
He was breast fed and never did he sleep

Sleep put him on Pam's breast
Breast would put him at rest

That is their son Malik

C.J. was always on the scene
Seen Brian at school he was not mean

Mean his Mom needed a man
Man named Brian took Pam's hand

Hand in hand their on their way
Making a home for Malik and of course C.J.

This was written over 12 years ago, unfortunately the G.
Family is no longer together but my love for them all is constant.

Happy Birthday Niece

Penny you blessed us with a baby GIRL
What took so long to deliver HER?

Aunty Pam was suppose to be THERE
I just don't know what happen to HER

Better late than never they SAY
Aunty Pam is here on TODAY

Penny, I prayed for you all night LONG
For labor for you I know is always STRONG

But God is faithful this is TRUE
He gave you a daughter and not a boy in BLUE

So count your blessings one by ONE
Girls are better any day then a hard head SON

Written for the birth of my niece Lakisha

Hazel "Bowers" Burton

September 21, 2005

I did not for get your birthday of this you can bet
But God had not provided me with finances yet

But having a Sister is awesome above everything
It is way better than silver or having a diamond ring

Having a Sister just makes my heart sing
Her name is Hazel what a wonderful thing

God made you and purposed you for such time as this
Giving me a Sister was always my wish

So now he has placed us almost next door
So we will spend many more birthdays for sure

So know that I love you and this love is true
And I'll never stop loving know matter what you may do.

Made especially for my Sister Hazel "Bowers" Burton
By her Sister Pamela Qualls aka pampoet
This 1st day of October 2005
Birthday was 21st of September 2005

I was raised with six brothers and "no" sister, a dream of mine of course
Was always to have a sister, and one day in the early 2000 I received
a call from a lady saying, hi I am your Sister Hazel," this call was the
blessing of my life as my father had told me that I had a sister 16 years
younger than myself, so I welcomed my Sister with open arms,
Love you Sister Hazel.

How Great Thou A.R.T.

How great thou A.R.T. is more than just a song
It is a person that encouraged me to continue on

On to prosper and on to grow
He is the REASON I told you so

Reason why I am not plagued with guilt
This brother has a line as smooth as silk

But he also has respect for his lady
I do not know her name, maybe it is Sady

But to this lady A.R.T. will be true
Regardless of what our bodies told us to do

He did not sow a seed into my water pot
See I was very weak and would not have said stop

But because of the greatness of God
A.R.T. decided not to use his lightning rod

True to his love true to his God
A.R.T. now has no REASON to duck or hide

See I was desperately lonely sometime in despair
This brother let me know that he was there

There to be loving there to be kind
There to respect me most of the time

So in conclusion his lady is very blessed
While she was away he passed one of lives hardest test

To be faithful to his lady friend
That is where this story will end

How great thou A.R.T. is more than a song
It is a person that encouraged me to continue to go on
1998

I Am A New Creature

I am a new creature in Christ you say
Why is it you always walk away?

Away from God's unchanging hand
Continuing to enjoy the sins of the land

Pleasures of this world come and go fast
Relationship with Jesus you'll learn to last

Fellowship with Jesus, sit at his feet
What my Savior will serve you; will be better than meat

He will give you peace of mind
In a bottle or drugs, peace you will not find

He will give you victory and hope
You won't be able to find this in dope

He will give you joy without measure
Open up the scripture you'll find in them treasure

Treasure more valuable than silver and gold
Keys to the kingdom let the story unfold

Copyright/TM /P.A.M
May 2, 1998
Pamela Qualls/Pamela Adkins-Murphy

I Don't Want To Fail You Lord

December 22, 2006

I've been hurt many times before
Even had church folk close the church door
Then in affliction you came to my aide
You said daughter you don't have to be afraid

This is a journey that you have begun
You live in the spirit with the father and the son
And when its all over this battle I've won
I don't want to fail you Lord
Don't want to fail you lord

My children don't understand
Although my husband does all that he can
But I will live and will not die
This affliction is because I am the apple of your eye
So when people come see about me
There is only one thing that I want them to see

When its all over and the healing is done
I don't want to fail you Lord

Valley Fever came knocked at my door
Body was aching and my joints were sore
You said many were the affliction of the righteous one
But you would delivery me cause you are the Son
So as the healing takes it's old good time
I only want people to remember, I was faithful and kind

When its all over and the healing is done
I don't want to fail you Lord

If I Could Not See!

2003

What would I do if I could not see?
Let's talk about it, let me see

Smiles on faces when passing by
I could not see them would make me cry

Upwords is my favorite pastime
No more playing I'd lose my mind

I love to read, this I could no longer do
I'd probably get to feeling blue

And then not seeing my ten grandsons' play
I could not imagine being blind any way

Then Taylor my shadow I could not see
She's my first granddaughter and she's only three

What would I do if I could not see?
I don't even want to consider how, that could be!

This poem was written when I was considering
the doctors report, not Gods lol
My ten grandsons are:
Willie III (Destiny), C.J.(Baby Trey), Wayne (Daeveon & Isaiah), Eddie,
Wesley, Marquis,
Antoine, Hezekiah, Patrick, Malik (new additions since
writing of this poem Timothy & Quentin
And one other beautiful granddaughter La'Trinity aka Angel Baby☺
Taylor my first born Granddaughter and assistant editor.

I Love You God-Mama-(P.A.M.)

God-Mother I really did not have much
Much for a gift so I thought I would touch

Touch your heart with love and joy
Joy we are hear another year old

Old to enjoy another Mother Day
Day of rejoicing and rejoice again I say

Say what's in the bag may be green
Green is a color meant for a Queen

Queen to all who know you well
Well is the place of health I can tell

Tell you always like to smell sweet
Sweet is in the bag knock you off your feet

Feet that are shod with the preparation of Peace
You God Mama are the first not Least

Least we forget to say we love you
You are the one that helps us not be blue

Blue is a way that sometime you may feel
Feel unloved and sometime ill

Ill from being in the house all alone
No one calling you on the phone

Phone up Jesus any old time
For he is a friend of yours and mine

Just remember your children do love you
And we are here tonight to tell you it too

Just be encouraged hold your head up high
Your heavenly home is way up in the sky

This is just a passing through place
I pray my poem puts a smile on your face

God Bless you God-Mama
D. Henderson
May 9, 199?

God-mother I met at the age of 80+, she was my pastor and after discovering I had never had God-parents her and her husband accepted me as their daughter, I accepted them back and was there for her and her husband until there end. She was one of the more classy women I have ever known, at the age of 80 she was still wearing high-hilled shoes. When I grow up I want to be just like her. Her legacy of "faith" she passed on to me and my husband calls me Madame Faith.

In The Cup!

It appears to be just coffee in a cup
U look inside and say "so what"

What is in the cup is not as clear
But the man who fixed it is always near

I know he loves me it's proved by the cup
Regardless of what happens with a cup we do sup

For everyday just like a clock
He makes my brew and never does he stop

Artificial hip and knee injury too
But with this going on I know what he will do

As everyday before he departs
Up the stairs he climbs and gives my heart a start

As in his hands is a wonderful cup
Filled to the brim as we must sup

Sup on Love and patience and care
When I see the cup I know he will always be there

So if you ever come my way,
Pray for the cup then U can say
He is a man in every way
Cause U can tell by the cup he's here to stay

Regardless of the weather summer, winter, spring or fall
I know that I am loved by the CUP and that is all

Made especially for my husband: Harry Jr. Qualls, January 6, 2007 By his
loving wife: Pampoet. I am so glad that I was able to express the way
I felt and appreciated all the small things that he did before his home
going on October 29, 2007. So all the little things that we do in life, can be
some of the most important and everlasting things that we ever do in life.

I Want A Man

I want a man, to hold my hand
Not be afraid to be a man

I want a man, to be mine all mine
Who is willing to spend some time

I want a man, who comes home at night
He won't fuss and he won't fight

I want a man, tender and kind
I want a man that can use his mind

I want a man, that looks his best
I want a man that can stand life's test

I want a man, to hold me at night
Kiss me embrace me hold me tight

I want a man, that walks real proud
Does not talk loud to draw a big crowd

I want a man, that is big and bad
I want a man, that is happy not sad

I want a man to pump my gas
Open my doors and allow me to pass

I want a man, that loves God first
Leads me to his car, takes me to his church

I want a man, who is sweet
Holds my hand kisses my cheek

I want a man, to run my bath water
Massage my back softly then harder

I want a man, to cook me a meal
I want a man, that won't think that a big deal

I want a man, to get to know me
I want a man, that will let me be

I want a man that will let me stand
I want a man, that can understand

I want a man, that can sing
I want a man, that can buy me a big ring

I want a man, that can cook
I want a man that can read the good book

And when this man does find me
I will be the best wife I can be

"CAUSE"

I REALLY WANT A HUSBAND
March 17, 1998

This poem has turned out to be a self prophecy.
I married that man in Ghana/Accra West Africa
In 2009. This man is everything that is mentioned
Above, not only does he love God, but this man
Can cook, read that book, and is not hard to look
This man is my husband Bernard, baby I love you!

I Want To Go Home To You

With ever raising sun and dim light rain, I want to go with you,
down, where your strawberries grow
Down, to where there is no snow, and sunshine vines spread row
upon

To sip the soil of sweetness, for the fruit that rest below
The fruit that rest below,
dark leaves which shade and shelter the ripening pearls of
sunlight

I want to go where the fruit is sweet
and has ripened slow with sweet, juices that run below

I truly desire once more for this rivers flow
with strange wavering river weeds
and watery shadows where sunlight bleeds
is just where I want to go

I want to go with you where test
are passed
and failed and even prayers can seem to rest
where no's mean yes and desires turn to tear drop at best

I want to go where time has no place
only roses, leaves, cinnamon drops and love filled hearts stay

I want to go with you down to the lowest place I know
under the field where the berries grow

Under the waters constant glow
away from the sun and rain and snow

Down to the buried bedrock layer
where the soil is solid as a mountain plateau

I want to go down with you where rock solid is all we know
and even desire to move on has to go

I want to fly where the wings of love, will blow us to and fro
and only time, can remind us, from where we are from

I want to go where tall trees begin to fall, and undergrowth
stands rich bushy and full
Where the roots are millions of years old, and the passion run
deep as the soul

I want to go with you where cry's for sweet JESUS become s
praise
and silly love never fades

I know in time as we pray
that our love shall never fade
and only time shall be cast away

I want to go with you until there is no more and even heaven has
become our open door:
I JUST WANT TO GO

I LOVE YOU QUEEN
Copyright@Alvin K.
permission to :P.A.M.
May 20, 1998

I Was Sick

Jesus said,"I was sick and you visited me"
See Rena this is the way it is suppose to be

I have been wounded in the army of the Lord
That does not mean I am suppose to keep score

I am suppose to do all I can do
Not to let forgetfulness happen to you

So I come with video in hand
Just to let you know I am Pam I am

Yes I love you this is true
You are my sister don't want you felling blue

So let's enjoy some coffee and fellowship
It will make you feel better and be warm to your lip

We will pray and ask God to heal
For we both know that this is his will

He wants us to prosper and be in good health
So that we can work and obtain our wealth

So by his stripes my Sister you are healed
And I am here merely doing God's will

You don't need medicine or a pill
You my dear need rest and to just be still

1998

Rena is my BFF, rider-or-die, or whatever one calls
A friend that sticketh closer then a brother or sister.
We have known each other for over 20+ years.

Jealousy

Why is jealousy oh so cruel?
Why it's because you're breaking a rule

A rule that tells you how to behave
It explains very simply, jealousy is cruel as the grave

It is so cruel you should see
It makes for artificial feeling between you and me

But you say you can't help yourself and you're trying so hard
Tell old jealousy to leave you alone and quit being on your guard

Resist the devil and make him flee
Then you can control that jealousy

Now that you know how to get rid of it
Don't ever have another jealousy trip

It will lock up your mind as if you're in jail
And make your life a living hell
JEALOUSY

12-02-84

Jesus The Only Way Of Salvation

Jesus is the way the truth and the life
God sent his only Son, no more hatred, envy or strife

He said "if you open your mouth and ask him to come in"
He will be your Lord and Savior and he will always be your friend

Confess him with your mouth, everywhere you go
Do not be ashamed of him let the whole world know

Confession with your mouth and believing in your heart
This is where your salvation will really take a start
Pamela Qualls
Copyright ©2007 Pamela Adkins-Murphy Qualls

John Beheaded

Mark 6:16-29

John the Baptist has been raised from the dead
That cannot be King Herod said

See John was put in prison by my order
He told me incest from God not a supporter

Herod had married his brother Phillips wife
John had said, "Herod you know that's not right."

So Herodias's anger began to grow
Biding her time then she would show

Show how powerful sin can be
When it has got a hold of thee

Herod found no fault in John
Righteous man he wanted him to live on

Then Herod had a birthday party and dance
Herodias daughter put him in a trance

Have half of my kingdom, anything you say
Give me John the Baptist head on a tray

Even though this made him very sad
He had to give the order that was bad, bad, bad

Copyright/TM@P.A.M.
Pamela Adkins-Murphy

Joined Church

Oh! I joined a wonderful church
I did not know if I belonged there first

First I must consult the lord
Always want to be on one accord

Told me this is the place for me
So I can grow in ministry

Ministry in music and song
Praising the Lord with G.C.M. all day long

Prophesied I was an answer to prayer
I know the Lord has sent me there

Then Athena came with me
Now my daughter has been set free

Free to prosper flow and grow
Encourage her husband don't you know

God has something in store for us both
As we continue to be led by the Holy Ghost

On February1, 1998
I joined Global Christian Ministries
Pastor/Dr. Irene Houston
Richmond, Ca
@P.A.M.i.A.M.
P.owerful A.nd M.ighty inChrist A M.inistry

Pastor Houston and my mother the late Pastor Franklin
Attending the same church when I was a child
Olive Grove Pentecostal Baptist Church in Berkeley, CA

As I am compiling my poetic works for this poetry book
I notice God has had me doing things that others are now
Doing, such as (will.i.am) God had given me:
P.A.M.i.A.M., with little I being me as God is the only
Big "I"

K.D. Bowe

02-04-99

Hallelujah K.D. BOWE
There are some things I want you to know

Came to Richmond California in a storm
This weather for us was out of the norm

But my daughter and I we were on our way
Wanted to meet K.D. Bowe (hold on now, look out) what you say

Your were MC for the release of a CD
And by the way you did meet me

My name is P.A.M. and my daughter's name too
I gave you a card it was white and blue

We must keep in touch this is true
My daughter is a singer, writer, producer and I sing too

So K.D. help give a sister a break
Let me read my poetry on the air for goodness sake

The public will be blessed and you the same
Look out Maya Angelou P.A.M. is my name

Kind & **D**ivine **B**rother **O**n-line **W**ith **E**veryone

Leeana My Granddaughter

July 15, 2007

My Granddaughter Leeana has long hair just like me
She is carrying my Great-granddaughter named Destiny

She came to our home a week ago
Where Willie was taking her she did not know

But she arrived to a home with much love and care
As her Granny Pam and Grandpa Harry will always be there

Her skin is creamy just like mine
Hold on one minute, you are on my time

Ok! she may not be black
If you look at her skin you will see that

But what she is, is more than skin deep
See baby Willie will worship her feet

For both of them have come a long way
To bless us with a baby one day

Many trials they have already overcome
But the two of them have the devil on the run

Soon they will marry and this is a fact
And I do not care what you think of that

As God made all colors red, white and blue
God made Willie, Leeana just like he made you!

My great-granddaughter was born October 20, 2007 (nine days before
her great-grandpa Harry died). Unfortunately her parents never got
married and the grandparents (my son and his wife) are raising this
beautiful little blessing.

Life Is Short

Life is short, you're here then you're gone
God forbid you let anger linger on

On in your heart on in your soul
Seed of rage your heart grows cold

Cold and callous as the night
Such a bad feeling it makes you fight

Fight the one who loves you most
Get in touch with God and the Holy Ghost

Life is a vapor here then you're gone
Gone to a place that life goes on

On to heaven Gods pure light
Off to hell if you continue to fight

Let the love of Christ shine in
Melt that callous heart give you a grin

Give you a heart of flesh not stone
Then you can love each and everyone

As Life is Short!

12-22-07

Lizards Everywhere

Lizards, lizards everywhere,
Here comes another one I do declare

I came to Africa just to see
A wonderful man getting married to me

I promised him to his home I would come
But if I saw a lizard I would promise to run

The first morning upon arising in my new home
A lizard on the kitchen screen, did I run?

No my husband ran him away
He said," come on Pam" I decided to stay

Lizards, lizards everywhere,
Here comes another one I do declare

Then to the bathroom I did go
Not looking for lizards this you must know

But as soon as out the house I did come
Looked on the ground where another lizard did run

A lizard here a lizard there
Another lizard I do declare

They come in many sizes and hues
So many lizards it could give you the blues

Instead of being angry and afraid
In my head a plan I had made

Embrace the lizards when they come
Then I would never have to run

Off to the shower I did go
Singing my song to God you know

When up on the roof what did my eyes behold
A yellow and orange headed lizard, now I told you so

**Lizards, lizards everywhere,
Here comes another one I do declare**

So I decided to embrace the thing
Although I keep them out of range

So off I went with camera in hand
Looking for lizards as I stand by my man

Saw a lizard on the brick wall
There was a whole family up there having a ball

As pictures with camera I did took
Believe it or not the lizards at me did look

Then as I shook my head and began to leave
Someone said take video of the Lizard, PLEASE.

So what I tell you is not a fairy tale
I have pictures I took them well
Lizards, lizards everywhere,
Here comes another one I do declare

Written in Accra, Ghana/West Africa
Pampoet/July 2009

Looking For A Love/Song

Looking for a love to last an eternity
Looking all a around but never inside of me

Never stopping to consider the love from up above
The one who gave his life for me and gives perfected love

Then I ran into it, it knocked me off my feet
It used me and abused me my spirit they did beat

See I was looking for a love to last an eternity
Looking all around but never inside of me

Then I looked real deep inside
What the world had told me was all a lie

Perfected love was not in a woman or a man
But holding on to the masters unchanging hand

Looking for a love to last an eternity
Now I know perfected love it lives inside of me

I will dedicate my life to him
He already gave his life for me

No more looking for a love that will last an eternity
I have found perfected love, he lives inside of me

Pamela Adkins-Murphy
12-02-98
I was inspired to write this poem/song by Pastor Reggie!

Malik 10ᵗʰ Birthday

Professor Malik 10 today you are
You my Grandson are a shining star

Your smart, your kind you're on the ball
You my Grandson will never fall

May the 23rd 2007 is your date
Granny has no money so your gift will be late

But with your Mom you will be
Also with your cousins, (Marquis)one, (Hezekiah)two not three

Of course your brother C.J. will be there
Just to let you know how much he does care

Princess Taylor your sister of course
Will celebrate with you not by force

Grandpa Harry said, "he would drop by
Granny could not be there but I will not cry

So go ahead and have a ball
Grandmama (Esther) is the mother of us all

Today is the day of your other grandma Glady's birth
You never met her as she passed on first

Made especially for you:
From your very own Granny Pam
May 23, 2007
Pamela Qualls; Phoenix, AZ

Marcellis 17th Birthday

May 8, 2000

Marcellis I have known you for quite a while
When I met you, you were just a child

Drummer boy was your nickname
Serving God your call to fame

I watched you grow tall as a tree
I'm glad God placed you with me

For I am your granny, aunty and friend
My love for you will never end

So as you turn the corner of life
Someday you will be someone's husband not wife

Remember all the values you have learned
Growing up turning into a man, now is your turn

Others have grown up before you
Other young men did not know what to do

But you have a foundation in Jesus Christ
This will be with you the rest of your life

Now I know I owe you 17 x Five
Why I said I would do this just wasn't so wise

But money is funny, I have no dough
$85.00 is to you what I owe

So keep this check don't cash it in
Cause if you do we will all have sinned

All my love
Granny-Aunty Pam

This is the first born of my best friend Rena. I came into Marcellis life when
he was five years old. God blessed his Mom to have three other children
"all girls" so Cellis gets the honor of being the only Son, and what a
wonderful son he has grown up to me, Cellis I love you and am proud to
have you call me, "Granny."

Marquis 7ᵗʰ Birthday

Marquis this is your 7th birthday
We are all here to celebrate

Your are grandson number six
Today your Granny was in a fix

Had to drive a long, long way
But I made it to your special day

Everyone was here for the fun
I was missing the only one

But that's O.K. that's all right
When you get your gift it will be all right

For thirty five dollars is $5 x7
It does not add up to eleven

For a gift you will take a ride
Not with a kite not with a bride

My name is Granny Pam I am
And yes I do like green eggs and ham

April 15, 2000
pampoet
People At Marquis Party

Mom—Patricia
Granny Pam and Grandpa Harry
Grandpa Willie aka PawPaw
Uncle Jr and Aunt Cardella
Willie III, Wayne, Wesley
Uncle Brian and Pam aka Auntymama
C.J. and Taylor
Aunt Melzena aka Aunt Eba
Edward, Antoine, Patrick

YOUR BROTHERS
HEZEKIAH AND GREGORY
UNCLE CARL, TIA AND KIARA, TATIANNA
$97.00

Master Plan Created

My husband is living far, far away
I expect him to join me most any day

Every day I look at the clock
Wondering when it will all stop

All the waiting is it in vain?
Will he ever get here driving me insane

But God said,"wait" and possess your soul
I have now turned another year old

Our Anniversary in a month will be
Will my husband at that time I see

Absence makes the heart grow founder
Distance makes a person wonder

Is this all a part of the Masters plan
Husband marrying me Granny Pam

He loves me and I love him too
We are so in love what can we do

But wait until the day does come
When at the airport into his arms I will run

My ways are not your ways
Just Love the Lord trust and obey

My thoughts are also different to
So just look and see what I will do

For in time you will see
What I have in store for thee

Exactly what I am going to do
Wait and pray like God told me to

Send your husband as quick as can be
Away from Africa to America he will see

See the great things God has prepared for him
For he has married me his wife his gem

07/10 by pampoet aka Pamela Qualls Botwe

After experiencing the tragedy of finding my husband dead at his computer, I went on the Internet looking for someone to talk to. I got a reply from a good looking African man in Ghana. We started talking and he talked me into being his wife with the declaration," I have finally found my rib." I went to Africa to ascertain this was real love and not a scam. We were married August 13, 2009, not knowing he would not be allowed to come back to America immediately as there is a long immigration process. All Praise to God we have endured a separation of over almost three years but it is coming to an end as he has finally obtained his VISA.

Met An African Brother

I went to the Bank of America today
I saw a brother standing there who looked A-okay

He had on an outfit that made him look like a king
I did observe he was not wearing a ring

He said, "his attire was from his home"
He asked for my number to call me on the phone

He said, "Nigeria was where he was from"
I told him I was sorry, but I had to run

He said, "maybe we could go to church"
As I observed his pretty silky green shirt

He said "Richmond was to far"
I said, "Sir do you have a car?"

So we were suppose to meet today
I did not see him something got in our way

But when he called me on the phone
He said,"he was there but I was gone."

So today we will try again
And possibly he will be my African friend

Heard men from Africa are one of a kind
Maybe God plans for one of them to be mine?

This is a true story and it happened May 4, 1998; God again was
speaking into my life prophetically. As I sit here getting my poems ready
for my first poetry publication I married an African man (Bernard) from
West Africa/Accra/Ghana 11 years later☺

Mother Blackman Gone Home

Today is a day of much regret
But we know God has never failed us yet

For he came to take his jewel home
Which will leave us all alone

But Mother Blackman gave us her son
Just like God gave his only one

She opened her home, where the first church was formed
She was always available to make us feel warm

She remembered me one day and brought me some shoes
I think of her kindness and I don't feel blue

Mother, sister, confidant, friend
She is still with us her spirit never will end

The way she dressed and carried herself
Her quiet spirit put her heads above the rest

We all knew this day would come
He searched the earth for Mother Blackman that special one

Satan tried to take her out before her time
But we all prayed and fasted and tapped into Gods spiritual line

He did answer cancer he did heal
And left mother here for many a year

She got to see part of her son's vision fulfilled
His ministry is dynamic and sick folk are healed

Even got to see grandchildren grow old
And become successful and wholesome and spiritually whole

The Lord did not stop there
But let her see Great Grandchildren his acts always fair

So she will be missed by one and all
Went home to be with Jesus; November 14, 1999 it was in the fall

copyright@Pamela Qualls/tm/P.A.M.
P.owerful A.nd M.ighty inChrist

Mother Land

Went to Africa aka The Mother Land
This for me was a part of Gods master plan

As I am Granny Pam I am
And one thing I know how to do is stand by my man

Now this man to me did find
Said,"he wanted a wife to make her mine"

But I said, "Africa is too far away"
So with this fellow I talked many a day

Then he said, "his rib he did find"
Ask me if I would be thine

After deliberating, doubting and prayer
God said, "this man for you would always be there"

So much to my wonder and surprise
The mother land is where this day I did arrive

My husband was there with a group of people unknown
This awesome greeting was in person and not on the phone

As in Africa the people are all fair
Wanted me to feel welcome when I did arrive there

When my husband saw me and I saw him
We knew we were meant for each other as we both did grin

July 15, 2009
Pampoet: Accra/Ghana/West Africa

Mother Who Are You?

Mother who are you? Mighty and strong
Holding onto the Masters everlasting arm

Someone who really cares
Tenderly you comfort and bear

Bear all your burdens problems and woes
Keep a door open so home you can go

Mother who are you?
Have I taken time to know?

Are you a friend or are you a foe?
Search your heart deeply and only then will you know

A mother is one who stands up to her task
Task of caring for her children all day
Task of teaching them all how to pray

Mother what are you?
Made of flesh or of glass

If I push you real hard will you be able to last
Last when the world has turned on you cold
And yet you can stand yet stronger and bold

Bold is who a mother is
Faithful to her child her life she gives

Gives with all her heart and soul
Soul of a mother grows hot not cold

Mother what are you, Mother who
Figure it out when I'm gone and your blue

This was inspired on the bus coming home from
A Smokey Robinson concert in Nevada, January 18, 1998
I had another negative encounter with one of my children

@P.A.M. i. A.M.
P.owerful A.nd M.ighty inChrist A. M.inistry

Mothers Day Tribute

Mother I just wanted to take time
Sit right down and drop you a line

Let you know I love you true
Regardless of what in life we have been through

Many valleys and mountains you have already climbed
Just remember to keep God on your mind

Me and my crew are on our way
To spend time at Clearlake on this Mothers Day

So even though if we don't see thee
In my heart is where you will always be

Your one and only daughter
pampoet and I know it

May 7, 1999

This Mothers day was spent with my oldest Son's
Other family, it was Wayne's birthday and we all
Went to Clearlake. I always loved and honored
My mother no matter what we went through and
We did have many challenges, but as we become adults
We realize we all do the best we can to raise our kids.

Mud Slides

Mud is sliding all around
Houses build on sinking ground

We must always count up the cost
When we decide to build that dream house

Build that house on a solid foundation
Then houses won't be flooded all over the nations

God intended trees to grow in the hills
Sliding houses gives owners chills

Animals can live in rain and mud
We shouldn't build houses high above

On the ground is where we can stand
Build you a house on solid land

Then when the storms beat on your house
You can give praises with your mouth

House is built on solid ground
Unlike houses sliding all over town

My 50th Birthday

Pamela Bowers, Murphy, Qualls, Hunter, Adkins

Dedicated to my 4 Wonderful Children and 12 Grandchildren

I thought it was much past time
For me to sit down and write a **thank you** rhyme

Thank you for making my 50th so grand
I am Granny, Mom, Daughter, Sister, and Friend named Pam

Pastor for taking out the time
Letting me know you and Leah are a friend of mine

To the Craytons family I am most impressed
You all showed up when you were enduring one of life's hardest test

Thank you all for the gifts you did bring
Money, presents and so many nice things

Thank you RENA for always being there
But on my day you showed me you really did cared

And then my sisters from my past
Vicky, Keva, Tonya, Pam and Betty came in at last

Thanks to those that could not come
But monetary gifts you sent me some

Thank you Mom for giving me life
Enabling me one day to be Harry Jr's wife

And most of all thanks to my "Trifling Kids"
It is for you my heartbeats and for you I do live

Pamela Ann Qualls

On my 50th Birthday day July 23, 2001 my children got together and gave me a surprise party that beats all. I had always said," they were Trifling" as special days come and special days go and sometime I might get a call and sometime not. Through the years on my birthday if none of my children do anything for me than me and my best girl Rere will do something for each other. This birthday was no different. My kids had no plans *I thought* so I made my own plans and almost ruined my surprise birthday celebration. So I choose to say what the word says," Children (Jr(Cardella), Eddie(Melzena), Pam-Pam and Pat), are a blessing and an inheritance from the Lord. I love you all my blessings.

My Sister Mitzi

Mitzi is my special friend
She is my sister till the end

We have seen many seasons come and go
But there is one season we both know

Season to show love for each other
We are Sisters we are not brothers

Weve both come through many storms
But Gods been faithful through every one

Help us hold our heads up high
Keep us looking to the sky

We will look to the hills which cometh our help
Jesus has never failed us yet

March 17, 1998

Mitzi is my spiritual Sister who encouraged me through the years and
when trials came she was faithfully with me to the end. My career in
poetry writing was encouraged by Mitzi and my poem," The Leaf of
Thanksgiving Eve" was financed by this dear Sister/Friend. We have lost
contact over the past twelve years. Mitiz, "thank you" and I will forever
love you and be grateful to you.

P.A.M.
Pamela Adkins-Murphy
P.owerful A.nd M.ighty inChrist

Naked-ness

Naked-ness is what you say
It makes many a person get on there knees and pray

David saw Bathsheba one nice warm day
Her naked-ness was showing he wanted to play

Looking at naked-ness caused a death that day
Sent Bathsheba's husband far, far away

Some people's naked-ness is beauty to behold
But not when you are Taylor and 3 years old

Don't let anyone see your naked-ness I say
I'm saying this to my granddaughter and her name is Tay

I tell her to her husband she can show
She says," Gran I understand, but not my Bro-Bro"

04-10-03

After being blessed with 10 grandsons's I was finally blessed with a
granddaughter; named Taylor. Raising a little girl with so many boys
around we must teach them the safety of not allowing anyone to see
them unclothed, so in the language that a 3 year old would understand
I would tell her not to let anyone look at her naked-ness. As you can see,
she most definitely understood. ☺

No More Pain

No more heart ache no more pain
Off to heaven is not a loss but a gain

Down here on earth always a fight
Defending justice could not sleep at night

Night would come and day brake at dawn
When I awake the pain is not gone

Always longing to get away from here
Going to heaven where there is no fear

What I see around me causes much pain
The way society is today I think I am insane

Guys with earrings, hair in braids
What this world has turned to makes me afraid

Afraid I have lived here on earth to long
So now it is time for me to go on

On to heaven a glorious place
Where you will see nothing but a smile on my face

Thinking about my mother
(Esther Mae Warner-Franklin)
on June 4, 2011 as she went to be with the Lord on December 18, 2010.

Pam's 31st. Birthday

To Pam-Pam my name sake aka Voice Of Meldoy

T'was 2 nights before Christmas and all thru the house
Not a creature was stirring not even my tired spouse

As I in my tiredness and your Dad in the bed
Had just settled down to rest our tired heads

And Willie and Eddie were all fast asleep
Cause Pat was not born yet to be under feet

When what to my wondering eyes should appear
It was warm, it was liquid and it was not root beer

So I ran to the room and a holler I gave
The baby was coming that 9 months ago was made

So we flew over to Kaiser Hospital quick as a wink
And to both our surprises what came out me was pink

Well Mother and daughter did not do real well
For I was in much pain and at times I did yell

Come doctor, come nurses come all medical folk
Come xrays and blood draws and all kind of pokes

So they discovered the ailment and I finally went home
Everyone was anxiously waiting by a phone

And my sentiments were the child brought me light
Gave a blessed Christmas to us all, now I'm tired and good night

Pamela Qualls

Copyright ©2007 Pamela Ann Qualls

This poem was written 35+years ago after this blessed event. Myself
being raised one of six brothers, I so desired a daughter. Having two
boys first and then getting a little girl was the highlight of my life. She
was born two days before Christmas, but she almost killed me lol; as I
had thrombosis in my legs (blood clots) hospitalized for five days, was
bedridden for two weeks after and medically had to be seen for months
after. This daughter became my daughter/sister/ friend that I never had,
and I thank God for her my name sake (Pam-Pam) being in my life.

Papa Joe Birthday 1983

Papa Joe after a day like yesterday today nothing could match
up.
Because yesterday was so beautiful it was surely tough-enough.

But thank God that this is your blessed day
For you were born on April 11, and not on a day in May

Billy and I didn't have very much money
Don't you laugh it isn't very funny

But we were able to come up with something very nice
You will enjoy it I'm sure because with it you use ice

Oh it comes in many shapes and colors
And some flavors are much better than others

Sometimes in a bottle sometime in a can
It really doesn't matter as long as I'm shared with all the clan

So kick back and enjoy your day
Open me up and say hooray

Don't worry about your dinner for that you've already had
Just pour me in a tall, tall glass and pretend that you are real,
real, glad.

All our Love: Billy, Pamela, Willie Jr. Edward, Pam-Pam, Patricia
and Cassandra

This is truly a poem from the past
as today is April 2, 1999 almost exactly 16 years later.
Since that time Billy has past but P.A.M. is here to last.
Did you guess what the gift was? Liter bottles of soda☺

Papa

Papa what are we going to do
Trying to express our love for you

We will pray and do all we can
We are your daughters Rena and Pam

We are so glad that God gave you Miss Mae
Standing by your side in every human way

Glad that she is special in your heart
Our prayer is that nothing breaks you apart

So by his strips you know you are well
Get up out of that bed and give the world hell

Made especially for you by your own God Daughter:
Pamela Qualls aka Pampoet
February 03, 2004

Papa the late C. Henderson was my God-Father. His wife the late D. Henderson was my pastor and god-mother. My best friend in the world is C. Henderson. She is my Jonathan and I am her David. This was written when God-Fathers health began to decline. Papa was a wonderful man and lived to be the godly age of 83.

President Barak H. Obama

Hope has truly come on the scene
He came as a President which is like a "King"

King said, "one day he had a dream""
That men would walk together nice and not mean

President Obama has walked through a door
That no one of color has walked through before

All of us can now feel we belong
As with Obama in the white house, we are no longer alone

Miracles we do expect of this man
I am sure he will do all that he can

Change and Hope is what he has given us all
As Michelle and President Obama has been on the ball

Our President is a man just like me
We come from humble beginnings; how could this be

God is our creator and we can go as high as we believe
Keep our President in your prayers when you bow on your knees

This is an original created document submitted to poetry.com
in Nov 2008

Pamela Qualls

VIP No.: P9145858
Book No.: 999

President Barak H. Obama is the first African American President of the
United States of America. His family consists of First Lady Michelle, and
first daughters Sasha and Malia and the first dogs name is Bo.

Prophesy

The Holy Spirit has anointed me to write
I won't fuss and I won't fight

Sometime I write all night long
Someday my writings will be turned into songs

Prophesy to the wind, "God Said"
Form your worlds as you write from your bed

Speak only positive things
Then anticipate the blessings I'll bring

All you're suffering was not in vain
During it all I helped you stay sane

If you suffer with me you will reign
Be on top and no more pain

Always Praise and exalt his name
P.A.M.ela your life will never be the same

P.A.M.i.A.M.
P.owerful A.nd M.ighty inChrist A M.inistry
Copyright/TM@P.A.M.
Pamela Adkins-Murphy

The reason my logo has a small i in the middle is because "i" as
insignificant but the "I Am" is what I am all about God.

Rena With Child

Rena, my sister, is now pregnant with child
She has not been this way for quite a while

Her children come in cycle of five
I tried to tell her this was no jive

So on her merry way she went
Not realizing the seed had already been sent

Sent to do the masters plan
Another child was his demand

So soon she will have another child
She has not been this way for quite a while

God does know what is best
My Sis. has endured many a test

But children are a blessing the Word does say
Why do so many men just walk away?

Yes! Paul has a nickel in this dime
He is going to work hard and provide this time

So it is all working together for their good
I ministered to them all that I could

But God knows best this is true
Just consider the Master in all that you do

Now on her face she wears a smile
She has not been this way for quite a while

Our beloved bundle of joy (Anna) was born December 9 1998,
the poem was composed 05/25/1998, unbeknownst
to me God was perfecting the Prophetic gifting within me
at that time, I am still a great work in progress

Ripen Tomatoes On The Vine

I looked over the fence and saw not cloths on the line
But beautiful tomatoes all ripen on the vine

I wanted to ask you and knock on your door
As mother and I had just come back from the store

You have not because not asking we do
So I ask Mom to go ask tomatoes of you

I gave her a few dollars for nothing is free
And said, "Mom you go ask, go ask and you see"

So off Mom did go with two dollars in hand
Leaving her daughter named Pam I am

You were so happy to give when she came
Went straight to the vine and blessed us in his name

For Jesus said, "by these signs men will know"
When you show love to others wherever you go

So thank you so much for ripe tomatoes off the vine
I am so thankful your are nice neighbors of mine

———————————————————❖❖———————————————————

Made especially for you On October 29, 2001
It is sad we do not know our neighbors anymore☹
My mother lived in East Oakland, and the next door neighbor
Grew many fruits and vegetables, this day while visiting Mother and I
had just come home from the store and forgot to purchase tomatoes,
when I looked out the side window and saw those beautiful tomatoes
"ripen on the vine", she was more than happy to share some tomatoes
and would not take the money, so I wrote this poem instead and gave it
to her. We became fast friends until she moved☺.

2007

The Egg

There is a little egg in a little nest
Patiently wanting to stand the test

The test of time that has passed by
Which makes the Hen at times cry

For she has a rooster oh-so-dear
One who she never has to fear

But he is waiting for the egg to hatch
He does not realize the Hen has a patch

But that old Hen is faithful and true
She'll hang in there until her face turns blue

For faith has changed the course of time
And this dear Hen is on the border line

For on that egg she must continue to set
All of her happiness rest
on the hatching of that egg I'd be willing to bet

Tagged

I went on the internet tying to get "tagged"
As the man I had met on there had truly made me sad

He became a liar, a con man, always seating on his seat
This was a man who I had to defeat

So after much praying, crying and then
Off to the internet I found myself again

Tagged was a place that I did not want to go
So I only put my picture and a profile to show

As I determined a man from God I did want
So getting back on the internet would only be more junk

But as I was getting ready to shut my computer down
I get an email "tagged" from a man out of town

I looked at his picture just as handsome as could be
This is exactly whom the Lord sent to me

As my original request was that he be black as the ace of spade
And this dear brother original man he was made

He is almost six feet tall
There was nothing else I needed this brother was on the ball

He said that he choose me from picture he had seen
Said I looked beautiful with a nice spirit not mean

And so we chatted and he thought I was heaven sent
When I told him I was 57 he asked exactly what I had meant

As on his profile he requested a woman from 37 to 24
How in the world did my 57 year old profile show?

He said you look to young to say that is your age
So he went back to "tagged" and guess what it said?

He is 33 did not matter my age he is in Africa looking for his
Queen
Said as Adam had Eve God to him his rib did bring

So we have been together for only a short time
But I believe in my heart that this brother is truly mine

Created especially for my love: Bernard K. Botwe
July 2009
Accra, Ghana/West Africa
This is how I met my beloved husband, "Bernard"

Trials And Testing's

Tried and tested on every **side**
Side hurts so bad you want to run and **hide**
Hide from pain that's all **inside**

Inside your body soul and **mind**
Mind your trials are not really one of a **kind**

Kinda puts your head in a tail **spin**
Spin round and round when will test **end**

End the sorrow and the **woe**
Woe begun were in a **war**

War against trials and **testing**
Testing to see if you'll faint or **sing**

Sing the praises of the **Lord**
Lord has it all on his **record**

Record the way you endured your **test**
Test to see if you would **confess**

Confess that he is Lord of great and **small**
Small little testing's should make you **fall**
Fall on your knees and call on Lord of **all**

All your trials and testing will **pass**
Pass when to Christ you turn at **last**

Last but not least to him if you **pray**
Pray and your trials and testing will not **stay**
Stay before God they will all go **away**

04/06/03

Valentine's Day 2009

Valentine's Day was the best day for me I could ever find
As I have a lover who is loving sweet and kind
I thank God above that this dear man is mine

The gifts started coming before the lovers date
My love wanted me to know our meeting was our fate

As the way we met was unusual to say the less
There were many others out there but my lover chose the best

One day I was delivered two bouquets of flowers brought to me
up the stairs
When I went to sign for them I was also handed a beautiful
stuffed bear

Oh I was so happy and it was not over yet
Another box with watch inside, knocked me off my feet, you bet

So after talking to this lover both day and night
He said he did love me and I had no need to fight

Then a few days later Valentine's Day was here
He said," Babe I love you and will always be quite near"

Well it started over again with a knock at the door
Another bouquet of floors almost knocked me to the floor

And while I was enjoying them another knock did come
This time to the door I hastened and did run

What do you think was in the messenger's hand?
12 long stem roses sent to me by my loving man

And while composed I did try to be
Another knock came to the door now this I could not believe

Now here is this great big box sent especially to me
I looked at it in amazement wondering another gift to receive

Well upon opening the box my eyes got really wide
As leather purse, belt and shoes were there to my surprise

So immediately I ran to the phone as this was more than I could contain
My lover said, "look real close as another gift still remained"

This had me baffled I did not understand
He said, "look in your mail box it was put there by mailman"

So to my mail box hurriedly I went
Only to open it and I won't give you a hint

Inside was a small box Lord what can this be now
Another red watch sent to me all I could say was,"WOW"

God has blessed me with a deserving man which is all I ever want
One that always puts God first now our life has just begun

My lover lives in Africa, and here to me he will come
He has asked me to be his wife as I am the special one
I told him that I would as this marriage to him would be fun

This was the beginning of the courtship of my husband who is in Africa. He is not a man of great wealth but spent everything he had showing me how much he loved me, and desired for me to be his wife. Upon my arrival in Africa he had done the same thing, sold his car and camera equipment to fix his humble home as if he was receiving a Queen, so anything that I can do for him I am happy to do as when he comes here to America to be with me, I already know he will be a most generous, loving and adoring husband. Mr. Botwe☺

Valentine's Day Poem

02-14-86

Hearts are red
I was feeling blue
Cause on Valentine's Day
I had nothing for the two of you

So, I thought and I prayed
And I prayed and I thought
And this is what my prayers brought:

A VALENTINES POEM

Valentine's Day doesn't mean a thing
When you receive rich chocolates and diamond rings

They may last long if you give it a try
Or just because you are happy, you may start to cry

But this can't compare to what's given by me
Cause you can keep this for eternity

It may get a little wet or might even tear
But in your hearts it'll always be there

From Pamela Murphy
To her Mom and Dad/Billy

Wedding Day

This is the day after my wedding Day
There are a few things I have to Say

God has been so good to Me
On the 25th December I married Billy

Oh he is such a wonderful Man
He's doing everything he Can
To make me happy he is my Man

He is so warm loving and Kind
I thank God that now he is Mine

And as our love continues to Grow
For the rest of my life with him I will Show

All my life with him I Give
For the rest of my life with him I'll Live

Look at Me
Oh if you could see my bridal Suite
Look! check it out, and say, "gee" that is neat

The décor is in my favorite color
Of course it is red and not another

There are mirrors on ever Wall
This suite is beautiful and I'm having a Ball

Billy has ordered breakfast for Me
He is now my husband don't you see

So round and round our lives did Go
Billy and my love continues to Grow

Billy and I were primary/elementary boyfriend and girlfriend. Married; December 25, 1984 after him being married to someone else and me being previously married also. We had not seen each other in over 15 years after we saw each other last at his 16th birthday party. What is meant to be will be? We were married until "death did us part" June 12, 1998

Wesley

BIRTHDAY #6
JULY 23, 1998

Baby Wesley this is your day
Like Burger King you should have it your way

You are growing oh-so-fast
That beautiful smile of yours will last and last

You are grandson number five
This is wonderful that ain't no jive

You are the youngest brother of three
Born on my birthday just for me

So be real smart, grow up to obey
Everything your mother and father say

You were born early in the morn
I started a prayer for you on the phone

For you were a very sick little child
But it only lasted a little while

I love you Wesley all the time
Always keep Granny on your mind

Made especially for you by Big Granny
P.A.M.

Baby Wesley was born by c-section July 23, 1992 especially for me on my 42 birthday, I had taken off work expecting to return as they were having a luncheon for me, but baby Wesley came out not breathing, after much time in ICU and hitting his small chest with those electrical shockers to start his heart, the doctors said," he was a little fighter but his living or dying would be determined over night, and he would be in the hospital for a few months". I got prayer going from my prayer group at my job (Social Services) and then I prayed over night for a miracle of healing. When I arrived at the hospital the next day after work, and went into the mother's room first, the baby was in the bassinet by his Mom. I ask what had happen, and Della Mae said," that over the night a miracle happened, and the baby was instantly healed". Today my Grandson is a healthy, happy 6ft tall young man. Healed☺

When I Met My Wife

I had just finished; to God, whispering a prayer
When I held my head up, my wife was there

I had just seen her walking across the lot
And when I saw her my heart almost did stop

Lord send me a wife; just like her
I'll hold her, love her and cover her with fur

And then like a vision my wife she was gone
I said, "Oh lord how can I go on"

And when I looked up what did I see
But this beautiful women in the car next to me

I ask her, her name and she ask me mine
I asked are you married she said, "no but I'm fine"

So a number from her I took right away
See I would not let my wife get away

Three hours later I gave her a call
I met her at the grocery store and not at a mall

We'll we did get married our life almost complete
But we will not be satisfied till we see little pink feet

So as our wonderful lives take on serenity
We will be welcoming our new baby, girl La'Trinity

This poem was made especially for:
Mr. and Mrs. Howard and Patricia
As told to me at dinner on March 14, 2004

When I See You

When I see you I know I can go on
When I see you I am no longer alone
Although I am always talking on the phone
When I see you I know why I was born
I see you when I am on the street
I see you when I look at my feet
I see you when I look at the sky
I see you when a bird goes by
I see you in my heart and soul
I see you everyday getting old
When I see you I know love
When I see you all Praise to thee above
When I see you??

Pamela Qualls

Copyright ©2007 Pamela Qualls

Of course this poem is talking about:

My Lord and Savior, Jesus. "When I See You"

Women with Issue of Blood-Mark 5:25-29

When Jesus crossed the lake by boat
Many surrounded him looking with hope

A synagogue ruler named Jarius came
Called out Jesus by his name

Come to my home as my daughter lies
Please come quickly I think she will die

Jesus began to move in the press
A women was there who needed some rest

Rest from all the twelve years of bleeding
Tired of spending all her money and pleading

If I could just touch the hem of his cloak
I could be healed like the rest of the folk

Then she reached out and touched his robe
Virtue left Jesus, his body grew cold

"Who has touched me" the Master said?
She fell at his feet as though she were dead

Daughter your faith has made you whole
Free from suffering as you grow old
Pamela Ann Qualls
Copyright ©2007 Pamela Ann Qualls

You Say You Want To Be A Minister?

You say U want to be a minister
But can God really trust him or her

For it is more than just wearing a name
If your behavior to the gospel brings shame

You want to be known and get respect
But your will to God U have not reset

For fruit of the spirit we need to see
How U treat others is what U need

U have a husband and possibly a spouse
Can they speak highly of U when you are in the house?

Actions speak so much more than words
With a renewed mind than U will be heard

So if greatness is what U want to do
Get on your knees and ask God to

Change your mind, attitude and desire
Then serving God U will go higher and higher

Wrote sometime in 2007, pampoet